THE EXPERIENCE SOCIETY

The Experience Society

LIFE BEYOND SUBJECTIVITY

SVEND BRINKMANN

Translated by Tam McTurk

REAKTION BOOKS

Published by
REAKTION BOOKS LTD
2–4 Sebastian Street
London EC1V 0HE, UK

www.reaktionbooks.co.uk

First published by Samfundslitteratur 2023
English-language translation © Reaktion Books 2025
Copyright © The author and Samfundslitteratur 2023

Tam McTurk asserts his moral right to be identified
as the translator of the work

This translation of the title is published by arrangement
with Samfundslitteratur, Denmark

The publishers gratefully acknowledge the financial assistance
of the Danish Arts Foundation

K:
Danish Arts
Foundation

EU GPSR Authorised Representative
Logos Europe, 9 rue Nicolas Poussin, 17000, La Rochelle, France
email: contact@logoseurope.eu

Printed and bound in Great Britain by Bell & Bain, Glasgow

A catalogue record for this book is available from the British Library

ISBN 978 1 83639 095 4

Contents

Introduction

The idea for this book came to me while I was waiting to board a flight at Copenhagen Airport. I nipped to the toilet and, on the way out again, a screen demanded to know, 'How was your bathroom experience?' Happy green smiley face, yellow neutral face or angry red glare? Unconvinced that it had been an 'experience' at all, I didn't play along. All I had done was answer the call of nature and wash my hands. How does that qualify as an 'experience'?

The fleeting, everyday experience confirmed something I had been mulling over for a while: that the very concept of the experience is now completely out of hand. Even I just referred to the memory as an 'experience', which is precisely the tendency I want to challenge. I could have referred to the recollection as an action or an event, terms that point outwards to the world. Instead, I wrote 'experience', which points inwards towards my subjective reaction to what happened, a key trend in what I call 'the experience society'.

Social scientists have a habit of labelling the times in which they live: late modernity, the consumer society, postmodernity, the performance society and so on. Do we really need another label? Despite the many important studies already conducted, I contend that a particular dimension of contemporary life remains under-analysed – the burgeoning trend to frame more and more of life as experiences. The concept has become so pivotal to understanding all sorts of phenomena and processes, including politics, work, education, identity, love, meaning and morality, that it justifies a more general analysis.

The book explores how this tendency manifests, in particular the psychological and ethical implications of living in an experience society. Not that the perspective explains everything. Of course not. It isn't some sort of all-encompassing category, but it does serve as a solid foundation on which to understand a great deal about contemporary life.

Several sociologists have discussed how we conceptualize and refer to more and more phenomena as 'experiences'. Gerhard Schulze and Steven Miles have both written books with the term 'experience society' in the title and linked the concept to the emergence of the consumer society.[1] I want to unfold the concept of the experience society and initiate a critical debate about the fact that more and more aspects of our lives are being turned into – and judged as – experiences. I want to analyse a key social trend critically, not just describe it.

One of my main criticisms is that turning everything into an experience means we run the risk of ethical impoverishment and alienation from the world because we constantly insert layers of experiences between individuals, and between people and the world. The upshot is that we no longer understand how to live more immediately. The prevailing narrative around experiences may sound present, warm and immediate to many people, but I would posit that the opposite is just as likely to be the case. Living in separate and individual worlds of experience rather than a collective reality alienates us from the world and each other.

Schulze introduced his thesis of the 'experience society' more than thirty years ago in *Die Erlebnisgesellschaft* (The Experience Society). In it, he identifies the tendency to turn life into an experience project as one of the critical features of modernity. A central principle of the experience society is that the value of something is understood based on the experiences it provides for the consumer. In principle, this applies to anything from coffee to love. Something is good if it is *experienced* as being good. Underpinning this new development is, of course, significant material and technological infrastructure, not least the vast 'experience industry', which encompasses everything from tourism to gaming and streaming services, an infrastructure that has only grown since Schulze wrote his book. In all sorts of contexts, what is most important is no longer how something *is* but how it's *experienced*. Significant aspects of the world have been reduced to our experience of them.

The Internet and social media, in particular, have added an attention economy layer to the experience society. The attention economy refers to the fact that human attention has become a critical type of capital. A whole host of digital-media conglomerates make their money by attracting and holding our attention, particularly on the adverts that fund popular services. That's why they compete for clicks, likes and the number of seconds a consumer's attention is fixed on a news item, advert or video clip.

The experience and attention economies are mutually interwoven. From the consumer's point of view, experiences have become a key commodity – computer games, music, social media, TV and so on. From the tech giants' perspective, the key commodity is the consumer's attention. We gain experiences by paying attention. That's the nature of the transaction, and it's not free, even if it doesn't always cost money. As so regularly and correctly pointed out, the consumer is the product when we access 'free' online services and exchange information, data and experiences. It is only 'free' because we pay with our attention, which facilitates targeted marketing of other experiences in an endless chain of experience consumption and attention harvesting. Often, we're not even aware it's happening. One of my aims with this book is to highlight and discuss some of the ways in which what I call our 'experiential life' is turned into an object, a commodity, which makes it subject to commercial and political exploitation. Once we are aware of this, we can hopefully act in a more enlightened and free manner in relation to the behavioural technology that underpins the attention economy. As philosopher Gert Biesta puts it, being a fully rounded individual requires the ability to 'direct one's own gaze; that is, to focus one's attention on some aspect of the world'.[2] Without this ability, we can't live freely.

On the other hand, digital trends are not the book's primary concern.[3] I will also analyse and problematize a number of other specific aspects of the experience society. First, I want to emphasize, more generally, that it privileges everything subjective. An experience is inherently subjective, and only the person having it is able to judge its quality. If my 'bathroom experience' at the airport was bad, it was bad for me, regardless of what anybody else might say or think. The more we talk about our lives in terms of categories of experience, the greater the risk of the objective world disappearing from sight. The experience society could, therefore, also be called the 'subjective society'.

Second, I will assert that the experience society may make it all too easy to disclaim responsibility by referring to experiences. This is essentially an ethical risk. For example, if an employee complains they've been treated unfairly, the manager may try to absolve themselves of responsibility by saying, 'That's all very well, but that's just *your* experience.' And maybe it is, but the experience might correspond to something that occurred in collective reality and was, in that sense, real. If we talk less and less about how the world is and more about how we experience it (feel, touch, sense and so on), then rational discussion ultimately becomes impossible because conversations are reduced to nothing more than a struggle for dominance between subjective experiences. I experience one thing, you experience another – end of story.

Argumentation that refers to the general, collective and objective gives way to the personal, particular and subjective.

Third, I want to show that in the experience society anybody can claim rights based on their experiences. If you feel bullied, you are a victim of bullying. If you feel offended, you are offended. Until the guidelines were changed a couple of years ago, the University of Copenhagen rules stated that something was deemed offensive if a person *felt* offended. This is, of course, highly problematic from a legal perspective, as it reduces the question of guilt to a subjective matter. Suppose my analyses in this book are valid. In that case, it suggests that the heated debates about identity politics and cancel culture in recent years are a superficial expression of a more fundamental cultural shift towards a subjective experience society. However, let me be clear: it is undoubtedly important to listen to and include marginalized voices and gain insight into the lives of excluded groups. Fortunately, that is becoming more and more common. But it's also important to meet each other in a collective reality and use a language that seeks to reach out to the world, not just inwards towards subjective experiences.

The book ends with an idea many will find provocative – that experiences may not exist at all. At least not as inner, private objects in our mental life. I will put forward and test the more realistic thesis that we live in a collective and real world, not just a world of subjective experience.[4] In other words, when we experience the world, we see real dogs, cats, houseplants, pizza boxes, motorways, sunsets and, of course, other people. Of course, we all do this in different ways depending on who we are and where we stand, but it's worth bearing in mind that when we arrive at an understanding of something, what we become aware of is not just a personal experience but potentially the real world.

So yes, of course, we experience things (dogs, cats, houseplants and so on), but it clouds our understanding to say that these experiences are, therefore, subjective. The fact that we can interact with the actual world also means we can be wrong about whether something was, in fact, a dog or a cat, an accident or an offence. We are not in this world by virtue of 'experiences' alone but with our whole mind, reason and living, moving bodies. Loving my wife is not about loving my experience of her. It's *her* I love. When I watch a funny film, it's the *film* that's funny, not my experience of it. When I drink coffee, it's the *coffee* I'm tasting, not my experience of it. The pop philosophy of the experience society is subjective and inward-looking. Nonetheless, since most of us grew up in this society, overcoming it will take something approaching a brand-new world-view and understanding of humanity (or at least a return to some of the thinking that prevailed prior to the psychologization of human beings). The project of drawing up a more realistic (and less subjective) world-view is beyond the scope of such a short book, but in Chapter Three I hope at least to point towards a possible escape route out of the prison of subjective experience. As humans, it would do us good to acknowledge we have a more direct relationship with the world than we usually believe is the case.

All this talk of experiences nowadays effectively doubles reality and can ultimately lead to us losing sight of the world, leaving us with nothing but purely subjective experiences. The fact that we have ended up here may also explain the incredible success my own discipline (psychology) has had in modern times in interpreting and improving people's experiential lives. One problematic aspect of the experience society is the pervasive psychologization of human life and suffering, a serious consequence of which is that we run the risk of ethics drowning in a sea of psychologized experiences. Regardless of your ethical standpoint, ethics must be based on the fact that there is something out there in the world – and not just in our experiential life – something for which we are responsible, that makes demands on us and of which we should take care. That is the book's core message.

1

Welcome to the Experience Society

I am writing this the day after the 2022 general election in Denmark. The prime minister, Mette Frederiksen, called it almost a month ago, proclaiming that: 'The 2022 general election will be about security. For individuals, for families, for your finances and in your everyday life. In Denmark, Europe and throughout the world.' Her short speech mentioned the Scandinavian concept of safety and a sense of security (*tryghed*) several times. She was addressing, among others, those voters 'too scared to go down to the laundry room in the block you live in because of delinquents plaguing your day-to-day life'. In short, she appealed to the subjective experience of a sense of insecurity, which is a highly tangible expression of the logic of the experience society. Who has not felt a little unsafe in or around the place they live?

Frederiksen (or her advisers) had perhaps read the Tryg Foundation's latest survey on the matter from 2021, which begins with the ominous words: 'Danes feel less secure', a conclusion reached because the proportion of Danes describing themselves as feeling safe and secure was at a ten-year low, compared to a ten-year high for a sense of insecurity.[1] A very large majority of respondents said that they felt less safe (or even far less safe) walking around their local area. Maybe that is what Frederiksen was getting at with her laundry reference?

On the other hand, it would have been better if the prime minister had gone into greater depth about the findings because – as the Tryg Foundation points out – the picture is somewhat contradictory. The subjective perception of insecurity may be rising, but the crime statistics, including for violence and threats, are actually falling. Søren Uhre, the head of the local police in the western suburbs of Copenhagen, where there is probably more of this kind of crime than elsewhere in Denmark, put it like this: 'It's a paradox that there is less crime, but people feel unsafe.'[2]

Why do people feel less safe when crime is falling? One answer might be that in the experience society we talk mainly about the subjective experience of feeling unsettled – especially when it is politically expedient. Objective reality is ignored. What do you say to a politician who declares: 'We feel the country has become less safe'? It's difficult because they're only describing an experience. You could, of course, point them towards the crime statistics that suggest the opposite, but in the experience society they simply don't carry the same emotional weight as appeals to the subjective feeling down in the laundry room.

Examples abound from politics of how the experience society revolves around the subjective. During the campaign mentioned above, the New Right proposed giving elderly people the right to say no to home helps who wear headscarves (in practice, Muslims) or are homosexual. Their reasoning was that it is important to feel safe in your own home. This is true, of course, but the fact such a discriminatory proposal was made and seriously discussed at all is indicative of a shift towards what is sometimes called 'emocracy', a system based on feelings, in which debate increasingly revolves around stirring up emotions, especially indignation, and in which the individual is encouraged to make almost unlimited legal demands on society based on their emotions.[3] It is less and less common for political leadership to be based on insights into the world that might help change how voters experience things and steer them towards facts.

In this sense, the 'experience society' is not just a term that denotes an age of tourism, consumption and mediated screen time. It is also an essential factor in modern politics and public discourse in general. The rest of Chapter One attempts to pin down what the experience society is, show how it manifests in key areas of society and demonstrate the fundamental relevance of the concept.

Politics as a Series of Experiences

In an emocracy, it is not only in matters pertaining to safety and security that subjective experiences take precedence. The same is also very much true of how voters view politicians. It isn't just candidates' policies that are presented and discussed during an election campaign, it's also their credibility. Trust in elected representatives is just as important as their ideological stance and policy platform.

We might ask what the point is of voting for somebody credible and trustworthy whose policies don't accord with your values and are against your interests. The trick is to make voters feel seen and heard, make them think the candidate is listening and acknowledging them. Conversely, is it preferable to vote for someone capable of implementing policies you agree with, even if your impression of them as an individual is negative? It might sound like the most rational approach – but not in the experience society.

Donald Trump is, of course, the high priest of this kind of politics, making the political process about experiences and shifting it into the territory of emotions and subjectivity. In his universe, what is important is not facts but experiences he can influence with his constant outbursts. Much of Trump's world-view can be traced back to the clergyman Norman Vincent Peale of the Marble Collegiate Church in Manhattan, which Trump's family attended when he was a child. Peale officiated at the marriage of Trump and his first wife, and the entrepreneur has often spoken of him in glowing terms. 'He was the greatest guy,' he said. 'You could listen to him all day long.'[4]

Peale, who died aged 95 in 1993, wrote arguably the most famous self-help book in history: *The Power of Positive Thinking*. First published in 1952, the book has sold millions of copies and is a kind of self-help gospel that contains the seeds of the experience society. The chapters have titles like 'Believe in Yourself', 'How to Create Your Own Happiness' and 'Inflow of New Thoughts Can Remake You'. The basic idea – regurgitated in countless other self-help books and self-development programmes – is that if you think positively and optimistically you can do almost anything. Facts are not nearly as important as how people experience them, and positive thinking can influence that. One chapter is titled 'I Don't Believe in Defeat' – a slogan Trump has taken to heart, as he is unable to accept defeat as an objective fact. If defeat is a state of mind rather than an objective reality, then changing your mindset (and seeking to influence other people's experiences) can ultimately make you a winner, regardless of actual outcomes.

We have all witnessed Trump's constant exaggerations and the unwavering belief in his own positive abilities that make him the embodiment of the experience society's political dimension. Not that his embrace of positive thinking extends to his opponents, whom he systematically belittles and mocks. It's all about him. The examples are legend. He lied about the crowd at his first inauguration (1.5 million, he said). During the 2016 presidential election campaign, he routinely welcomed 'thousands of people' to rallies despite the small size of the crowd. Turnouts did pick up later in that campaign, however, perhaps because of the self-fulfilling prophecies to which he believes positive thinking leads. Positive thinking taught Trump the mind creates its own reality. If you repeat 'alternative facts' often enough, reality bends to them and to your advantage – or at least you persuade people to believe them.

We don't have Trumpism in Denmark, thankfully, but an equally subjective understanding of politics rears its head from time to time. In 2017, when Peter Skaarup was still in the Danish People's Party, he made a remarkably clear statement in its *Ugebrev* (weekly newsletter) under the heading 'Politics is first and foremost emotions'. In a subsequent newspaper interview, Skaarup explained: 'I believe facts are subordinate to opinions and feelings . . . it would be good if some discussions were on a non-factual basis.'[5] He admitted that 'facts are interesting and an important concept' but very curiously added that 'they are not necessarily the truth.' It remains unclear what he thinks facts actually are if not the truth. However, according to the emocratic politicians of the experience society, truth is more likely to be found in the perception that 'everything is wrong' (in the case of the Danish People's Party, about immigration in particular – no matter how much controls have been tightened in recent decades). Something could actually be wrong, of course it could, but it's difficult to imagine how anybody can substantiate this by referring solely to emotions and excluding facts.

At face value, Skaarup's words reflect a pretty radical – even dangerous – irrationalism and entail the risk of reducing politics to just the art of seduction. It is probably no coincidence that Skaarup has since fallen in with the Denmark Democrats, whose leader, Inger Støjberg, persistently tried to change the public's perception of her infamous transgression while serving as a minister by referring to it as the 'child bride case'.[6] Støjberg defended her breach of the ministerial code, which led to a historic ruling against her in the Supreme Court, by portraying herself as a heroine, complete with personal iconography in the form of a logo featuring her characteristic bun of red hair. Attempts were made to use loud and emotionally driven appeals for indignation (about young refugees) to drown out objective discussion of a minister deliberately flouting the law. In all fairness, it might be added that the resentment whipped up towards Støjberg's person was also fuelled by a kind of emotional vicious circle.

Of course, emotions have a legitimate role in politics, whether associated with enthusiasm or indignation, but they should never be detached from the facts. Some people may feel frightened when they see a group of people with a different skin colour coming towards them, but it is legitimate to criticize an immediate reaction like that if it's based solely on unfounded prejudice. Fortunately, while it might not be easy to change, having a better understanding of a situation often helps us feel differently. Facts can change our emotions – as long as others are willing to enlighten us. In a democracy, that would be the media, social scientists, elected representatives and anybody else with a good grasp of the issues who wants to chime in. In a pure emocracy we are left to our feelings and experiences. I am not claiming that politics without emotion is desirable. That way cold, dispassionate technocracy lies. Nor do I think we live in a pure emocracy. The formation of the historic multi-party coalition government across the centre ground following the 2022 general election in Denmark actually points in a different and more technocratic direction. Having said that, it's worth noting that the 'necessary reforms' the new government advocated were repeatedly justified by emotional appeals to people's experiences of crises Denmark faces as a society, several of which seem to have been exaggerated. For example, six months after the coalition took over, the 'economic room for manoeuvre' suddenly and dramatically expanded. In other words, the economic crisis wasn't all that real – it had just been imperative to make the population believe it was. Justifying everything on the basis of experiences is a tricky business because they can be as fleeting as a summer shower.

I started this chapter with a closer look at politics because, in my view, the experience society is at its most dangerous when the political process is reduced to the subjective art of seduction. I will now turn to a brief discussion of other areas in which the trend towards referring to experiences all the time has made inroads.

Working Life as a Series of Experiences

Work is one of the most significant arenas of human life to be framed as experiences in recent decades. No one so much as bats an eyelid at the idea that employees need to supplement their professional qualifications with personal qualities. Staff are routinely expected to be flexible, adaptable, resilient and happy, and to possess a sense of humour – qualities often associated with the experience of meaning and involvement.

Linking emotional involvement so strongly to work is not a new phenomenon. Ever since the emergence of the 'human relations school' of psychology and industrial sociology in the 1930s as a reaction to a previously highly mechanical view of work, considerable interest has been shown in workers' subjective experiences of well-being, motivation and meaning at work. In the twentieth century, human relations metamorphosed into human resource management. People no longer sold just their time and objective skills as labour (as documented by qualifications, for example), but also their personal, social and emotional competencies, which were subjected to monitoring, quantification and optimization as well.

Job adverts have changed drastically in the last half-century to reflect the new demands. Employers used to seek reliable and conscientious staff, but now they look for innovative, passionate and positive individuals capable of providing good experiences and triggering positive emotions in themselves and others. Specific abilities and skills are no longer enough.

The modern workplace is also increasingly organized to provide a good 'work experience'. Big multinationals hire 'chief happiness officers' to generate job satisfaction. Employees are made to feel connected with their workplace because of a range of benefits and activities previously considered part of private life – sports and fitness, excursions, lectures and much more. In some workplaces, colleagues are almost a second family. The businessman and philosopher Morten Albæk, who deserves credit for rekindling the debate about living meaningful lives, has even argued that we should learn to love each other in the workplace. Albæk informed the Danish trade union magazine *Djøfbladet* that he has told several employees he loves them.[7] He advocates 'meaningfulness reviews' with staff because, he says, employees who experience meaning in life are five times more productive and take significantly less sick leave. In the experience society, the experience of meaning is a productive force for improving the bottom line.

The desire to introduce love and meaning into the workplace makes Albæk the latest in a long line of businesspeople who advocate breaking down the boundaries between private intimacy and professional activity, and turning inner experiences of meaning and value into tools for productivity and optimization. The trend took off in Denmark a couple of decades ago after the publication of *Corporate Religion* by the advertising executive Jesper Kunde. The book introduced the idea that we should elevate the belief that what your company does is both right and profitable to a 'religion, a management tool to which everything in the company is subjected'. Kunde asserts that employees should see themselves as missionaries and that there is only room for people who work with them, not people who work against them.[8] Five years later, the Buddhist businessman Christian Stadil and professor of management studies Steen Hildebrandt wrote *Company Karma*, which seeks to spiritualize our relationship with work. In one interview, Stadil said it's only when we let go of ourselves – by entering a trance or performing other spiritual practices, for example – 'that we perform optimally'.[9]

Statements like that are not exactly common parlance in manufacturing companies out in the boondocks or in cleaning companies, although companies in both these sectors have tried to cast work as a creative, almost spiritual experience. Nonetheless, business gurus like Albæk, Kunde and Stadil have had a significant impact on the public debate about our relationship with work, which – for better or worse – is increasingly seen as a space for meaningful experiences, emotions and self-development. Work is not just about *doing* something, about performing certain duties for which you are paid, but about *feeling* a certain way while you do it.

In the industrial society, love, religion and meaning were private matters and had nothing to do with work. In the experience society, we see the breaking down of this divide between the private and public, even at work. In my eyes, bringing meaningfulness reviews and love into the workplace is indicative of the boundless technique of intimacy that puts even more weight behind the 'tyranny of intimacy' described by the sociologist Richard Sennett in the late 1970s.[10] It is a technology that seeks to embed management and work even deeper in our consciousness, and we run the risk of instrumentalizing existential meaning by linking it to productivity. The sociologist Eva Illouz calls this 'emotional capitalism', as emotional experience itself becomes a form of capital.[11] The problem with this, of course, is not that people have emotions but that their inner emotional experience becomes a resource to be optimized and quantified as a key performance indicator. The value of emotions is reduced to what they deliver on measurable parameters.

Health as a Series of Experiences

If there is such a thing as a religion in the experience society, it has to be health. The philosopher Morten Ebbe Juul Nielsen wrote *The Health Diktat* because health is worshipped like a deity in his eyes.[12] When people are no longer part of a greater order outside the self, they focus on optimizing what is inside them, which quickly becomes a kind of health rat race, the goal of which is to accumulate as much health capital as possible.

Back in his day, Søren Kierkegaard looked at the pursuit of good health in his analysis of what has value from an aesthetic perspective. The term 'aesthetic' is closely related to the word 'experience', as it comes from the Greek *aisthanesthai*, which means to feel or sense. Kierkegaard described how the aesthete, who lives for exciting, varied experiences, lacks a broader horizon of meaning (or, in his terminology, something 'spiritual') to guide their life. Therefore, the only possible direction for such an individual's existence is determined by their psychological constitution. 'What do I want?' is the aesthete's basic question. The basic value of existence is to enjoy life, and as such health becomes 'the most precious good . . . that around which everything revolves', as Kierkegaard put it in *Enten–Eller* (Either–Or).[13]

In an aesthetically oriented experience society, health represents surplus value because feeling good becomes the most important aspiration. Am I happy? Am I relaxed? Glad? Free from pain and symptoms? Fit and thin? I'll just ask my fitness watch or self-help app. These are typical questions asked by modern human beings. They are not foolish or unimportant, of course not, but they are undoubtedly inward-looking, which means they may well lead us to forget the external life in which we interact with others. In the experience society, external actions are often seen as tools to maximize positive, inner and healthy experiences. In that sense, it is a bit of a paradox that we need objective indicators from watches and apps to evaluate experiences, which are supposed to be subjective.

I recently gave a presentation to a local authority that had launched a number of initiatives to improve the mental health of children and young people. As befits the zeitgeist, the council's incredibly sympathetic concept of helping others was justified by the improvements it would make to your *own* mental health. The message is that being a good person is good for you. It is a strange logic, which relativizes doing good to a subjective benefit for the person doing it. In Kierkegaardian terms, ethics becomes an aesthetic matter.

We also see here the same inherent contradiction regarding health that we saw earlier, in the example of the political speech about not feeling safe. We are constantly encouraged to monitor our experiences of stress, discomfort and pain. Objectively, human health has improved dramatically in the last century, yet our subjective experience of it has deteriorated.

Professor Arthur Barsky MD calls this the 'paradox of health'. More and better methods of diagnosis and treatment mean people check their symptoms all the time, leading to mass subjective discomfort. In short, the more advanced medical science becomes, the sicker people think they are.[14] The safer society becomes, in an objective sense – in terms both of crime prevention and of disease detection and treatment – the more unsafe and unhealthy people consider themselves. This is an unintended consequence of the experience society, but we must also bear in mind that major political and economic interests feed off of us feeling afraid and insecure. These emotional states create the need to safeguard, quantify, weigh and optimize our health. They create the demand for politicians or companies that promise to alleviate our sense of insecurity. In the experience society, we are willing to pay through the nose for the subjective experience of feeling safe and sound.

Identity as a Series of Experiences

One concept to make a strong comeback in public debate in recent years is identity. Originally meaning 'the same', it came to the fore as a psychological concept after the Second World War. The developmental psychologist Erik H. Erikson was one of those who linked it to adolescence, a time when you were supposed to 'find your identity', which is then more or less fixed – or at least, so they thought in those days. Identity was to be found at the intersection between what a person wants to be and what the world will allow them to be.[15] In this perspective, you are who you are because your wishes and endeavours are tempered by objective facts. Identity isn't just an experience. It is also related to an external reality outside the realm of subjective experience.

In the experience society, the objective dimension of identity has become less important and may even be in danger of disappearing altogether. I no longer have the same identity as a result of being the child of certain parents, part of a particular family or born in a specific region. Instead, I am who I *experience* being in terms of gender, values and duties. Identity is now more about what you subjectively *identify* with and less about external, objective roots and connections.

Arriving at this point is the culmination of a long process in intellectual history that began in the seventeenth century with the philosopher John Locke. He believed that what makes a person the same over time (and therefore identical to themselves) is not something physical found in the brain, body or external material conditions, but the chain of memories that links past and present. In short, I am the same because I have an experienced memory of my life. Locke argued that if a prince and a penniless cobbler fall asleep, and their memories are magically swapped, then we – and the characters themselves – will consider the prince to be the person in the body of the cobbler, and vice versa. According to Locke, this is because we use subjective psychological factors (memories from our lives) as criteria for personal identity. This suggests that we can also change our identity by changing our psychology. In principle, we can be anything we want if we change how we think about ourselves. It is a short step from here to the most extreme version of the 'you can do and be what you want' mindset so dominant in recent decades, and to the life coaches who claim that only 'obstructive beliefs' stop people from realizing their true potential. Suddenly, we are close to Trump's idea that we can create our own lives by using positive thinking to change how we are experienced.

But what if identity is something more given and less experienced? What if I am who I am by virtue of my objective ties to other people – no matter how I might experience them? For example, being father to my children very much defines my identity – even if being a father is not just an inner experience but a fact. In the experience society, if the importance of these identity-defining facts is downplayed or disappears, the fear is that we may become unable to understand ourselves because we believe that the truth of who we are must be sought in inner experiences rather than objective relationships and contexts. Ultimately, we would lose the ability to fulfil our obligations to others if we believed that such obligations only exist if we experience a sense of them.

Meaning as a Series of Experiences

I have already mentioned one of the most important concepts subjectivized in the experience society: meaning.

We talk a lot about meaning in innumerable contexts. We have already encountered 'meaningfulness reviews' and many of us yearn for a meaningful job. Learning should be meaningful, going to work should be meaningful, relationships should be meaningful, and people seek out voluntary work for the same reason. However, in my opinion, the typical concept of 'meaning' is too narrowly linked to the subjective and to experiences. It is difficult to prove this because the concept of meaning itself is so loose and used in so many different ways, but often it's used to describe something meaningful *to me*. If I *experience* that something has meaning, it *has* meaning.

On the other hand, a purely subjective concept of meaning is a flimsy one. It is not just an individual experience that makes something meaningful. We can, of course, discover that something is meaningful in a way that we might not have initially realized. We can become wiser and learn more about meaning. Learning a new language is an example of this. At first, we don't understand a word and can barely distinguish where one ends and the next begins. However, as we learn the new language, we discover its meaningful structure as expressed in words and sentences. Often, it is in practical contexts that we learn these things best. Consider the four letters that make up the word 'pain'. While it looks the same on paper in both English and French, the meaning becomes apparent, for example, when an English speaker is writhing in agony and shouts, 'Help! I'm in pain!' or when a French speaker points to a baguette in a boulangerie. The point is that words only have the meaning they do because language users have a fundamental consensus regarding how they should be used.

The idea that the meaning of language is linked to how words are used in practice was a crucial point in the twentieth-century philosophy of language, especially that of Ludwig Wittgenstein.[16] Words make no sense if they refer to something private and known only to the individual speaker. If that were the case, words would be deployed randomly, rendering communication impossible. Words don't derive meaning from referring to inner, private experiences but from being used to denote common, observable phenomena, such as a person's visible signs of agony, or bread in a bakery. In other words, linguistic meaning is linked to collective practice, not subjective experience. This is an essential requirement for words to mean something and for language to have meaning.

Imagine the same was true of other types of meaning. Existential meaning, for example. The idea may be hard to grasp for those of us who have grown up in the subjectivist culture of the experience society, but it is worth considering whether the meaning in our lives, in our activities, in our obligations and moral demands and so on, could be linked to collective practice rather than just to something internal and subjective. I explored this idea in my book *Standpoints* – my term for the phenomena in our lives that have inherent value and fundamental existential meaning for us.[17]

One phenomenon often – and rightly – associated with meaning is love. As an unconditional devotion to something other than yourself, it is very much a standpoint. People even say that love is the meaning of life. That rings true to me, but in the experience society love is often reduced to an experience, which is a harmful way of looking at it and is based on the idea that loving somebody else is an inner state of experience. If that were the case, when someone asks, 'Do you love me?' the other person might answer, 'Oh, I don't really know. I'll have to examine what I am experiencing first.' That's not how it works. Inner experiences – feelings, sensations and the like – are no guarantee of love. When we love other people, we love them even without that kind of inner experience. When I am at work and immersed in a project, I am not aware of my feelings, but if I were suddenly asked, 'Do you really love your wife and children?' the answer would, of course, be 'Yes.' I know this without having to search my feelings first.

The experience society has turned love into an inner feeling. Of course, I don't deny that love is often accompanied by emotions such as happiness, pride and joy, but it also comes with more problematic emotions such as jealousy, anger and fear. The point is that love isn't made up of such feelings per se but of the devotion inherent in your relationship with those you love. Saying 'I love you' isn't a matter of reporting on an inner experience but an expression of that devotion. Saying 'I love you' is what twentieth-century philosophers refer to as a 'speech act'. Love isn't a private experience but a phenomenon that manifests in people's shared lives and actions. Believing love exists only if we are experiencing it and feeling it all the time inside will quickly drive us to despair as we seek in vain to find fleeting feelings that naturally come and go. Fortunately, the meaning of language and love exists even when we don't feel the phenomena as inner experiences. Love and meaning are more than just experiences.

Technology and Media

One could easily write a whole book on the technological underpinnings of the experience society. Many of us spend hours every day immersed in the Internet, social media, streaming services and TV. You would think we would hanker after a break from the screens that dominate working life, but apparently we are so accustomed to a life mediated by technology that we relate to the world through our experiences on small and large screens at home as well as at work. Data from the Health Authority in Denmark shows that it is not only among adults that screen time is on the rise. It has been the same for all age groups over the last decade, especially young people. For example, one in four fifteen-year-old girls spends at least four hours on social media every day, and one in three thirteen-year-old boys spends at least four hours a day (Monday to Friday) gaming. At weekends, the numbers are even higher.[18]

Researchers, health and education professionals and parents have myriad different opinions about this trend and its ramifications for well-being, self-esteem and even mental health. However, it is important to adopt a nuanced approach to the debate because not everything on a screen is passive consumption of experiences. Many people, including children and young people, use the Internet to learn languages, engage in political discussion and seek out virtual communities of like-minded people in which to pursue all kinds of interests. Although I am not an alarmist about the trend, it is also important to be aware of how the smartphone-driven world of fun and entertainment has colonized our lives, as Steven Miles gloomily describes in *The Experience Society*.[19] Nowadays when people have to wait five minutes for the bus, they usually pull out their phones, and the time for reflection, or even for a bit of tedium, is filled with screen-mediated experiences. We don't know how this will affect human-kind in the long term, but it's telling that so many people seem to yearn for a time when external stimulation wasn't so intense and unrelenting. When people are willing to pay handsomely to go on a retreat without a phone, perhaps it's a sign that they need a break from being constantly bombarded with experiences.

Even before screens started to invade every part of our lives, cultural analysts were already writing about how the directly lived life is increasingly being replaced by representations.[20] In an age of consumerism, the immediate life becomes the mediated life. Tourists no longer just take photographs of the places they visit but selfies, making themselves part of the experience repre-sented. We use social media both to communicate and to experience ourselves. We don't merely present ourselves to others, but 'curate' ourselves as if we were on display in an art museum. On top of that, museums themselves are now a prime example of turning everything into an experience. The focus is no longer just on *Bildung* and enlightenment but on providing experiences for visitors, typically mediated by digital technology. The history of the exhibited objects is becoming less important than how they are communicated through narratives and visual dramatizations of historical battles or Viking raids. If the experience is less than enthralling, press the boredom button and that's them told. I have given talks after which the audience was invited to press a green, yellow or red button depending on how entertaining they found it. I, for one, didn't find the experience edifying.

How Did We Get Here?

To round off this whistle-stop tour of different corners of the experience society, it is worth asking the question: how did we get here? So far, my approach to this society and its subjective logic has been largely descriptive. I have tried to illustrate how significant social arenas related to politics and working life and existential issues of identity, meaning and love have ended up revolving around experiences. One way to express this is to say that what Kierkegaard described as the aesthetic in a human being – that which relates to our experiential life – now takes precedence. This is what we seek to fill our lives with, as exemplified by the discussion above on health, and this whole trend is materially underpinned by technologies that mediate experiences and are linked to the attention economy. But how did all this come about?

When we talk about profound social shifts, there is never a single answer to that question. We have to take into account all sorts of developments in intellectual history. Humans used to understand themselves as living in a world of objective meaning and value that they could use to orient themselves and base the way they lived. In his excellent book on the emergence of the modern self, philosopher Charles Taylor calls this an 'ontic logos' – a larger cosmic context afforded by nature, God or historical communities.[21] There was a meaningful context outside the self, which the individual had to know, connect to and live in. However, the ontological breakthrough of modern science 'disenchanted' the world, as the sociologist Max Weber put it. Nature became a mechanical system of causes and effects. We no longer found purpose, meaning or value in the external world. Instead, we attributed these phenomena to a newly discovered inner world of experiences.

In ancient Greece, in the epic poems of Homer, for example, the important things in life are found outside the individual. Specifically, they take the form of gods and goddesses, who appear during times of conflict and when difficult choices need to be made. Gradually, however, the notion emerged that everything important is found inside the individual – my inner self holds the truth about who I am and what I must do. The gods were rehoused in the self, driven out of the external world, which became the object of neutral, scientific description. As Galileo said, the book of nature is written in the language of mathematics. In other words, everything that could not be understood mathematically and quantitatively – everything moral and existential – moved into the subjective space and was made into an experience.

This shift was particularly pronounced during the seventeenth-century transition to modern philosophy, most clearly represented by René Descartes. The famous French philosopher postulated that, as sentient beings, we are not in contact with the world as such but only with an experience of it – at best, a faithful copy, at worst, an illusion. In principle, we have no way of knowing whether our experiences correspond to something in the external world or if other people are experiencing the same as we are. In principle, I can't even know that other sentient beings exist, which is the logical – albeit rather absurd – end point of the philosophy of experience known as 'solipsism', according to which the individual believes they are all that exists, locking them into a prison of their own experience. While modern cognitive sciences such as neuroscience and psychology explore human knowledge in a more sophisticated way than Descartes, the research often rests on the same philosophical foundation – that we are not in contact with the world as such, but only with 'mental representations' (as they are now known) of the world outside the self. The language is different from that of Descartes, but the philosophical problems are, unfortunately, the same. I would argue that these problems are inevitable as long as we take our starting point in the doubling of reality for which experience thinking paves the way. In the final chapter of the book, I will present an alternative, in which humans are not just *experiencing* beings but *acting* ones, who exist alongside things and other people in a shared and knowable reality.

In parallel with the ideas that emerged from disenchantment, we have witnessed a historic shift in the last century from an economy centred around production to one that revolves around consumption. In the consumer society, the focus is not just on producing good, cheap products but on triggering lifestyle aspirations. This desire is fuelled mainly by advertising and marketing – which, according to Miles, have become inseparable from the products they sell, just as consumers (all of us) have become inseparable from our experiences. To own material goods like property and cars is to own a certain experience. When you buy a product, you also buy a story about yourself. In a prosperous country like Denmark, virtually every home is warm, safe and fully equipped with all mod cons, and almost any car takes you wherever you need to go. So why not just stay somewhere cheap, even if you can afford more? Well, there is a crucial difference in the experience of owning one thing rather than the other. Put simply, we are what we experience. There is a difference between the experience of owning a house in Belgravia and one in Northumberland, even if the two houses are the same size and have the same material facilities. Why not just buy the cheapest car, which can do 110 mph (175 kph), instead of a far more expensive one that does 150 mph (240 kph)? The motorway speed limit is 70 mph (110 kph), after all. The answer lies in the experience and self-esteem associated with owning the expensive one – at least, if you belong to a demographic that values such things. In other contexts, owning an expensive car (and perhaps driving in general) may be seen as superficial and a waste of resources.

The experience society is the result of a fundamental economic shift towards the intangible. When we no longer have any fundamental philosophical understanding other than the basic claim that humans are just beings having experiences, we end up with a problematic alliance between ideology and economics from which it is extremely difficult to break free. Nevertheless, in the rest of the book, I will attempt to show that there are other, more valid – and more human – ways to look at life than restricting yourself to defining everything as categories of experience.

2

But That's Just How
You See It

Chapter Two explores two typical ways in which the concept of experience is used in discussions about power and morality. At first glance they seem to be completely different and point in opposite directions. One of them dismisses criticism by saying it is just how the critic experiences the situation; the other makes the criticism indisputable by making a negative experience absolute. My thesis is that both reflect the same problem in the experience society – that the concept has become a central focal point in discussions about what is right and reasonable, at the expense of references to the collective world in which we all live together.

One of these common ways of deploying the concept might be dubbed 'experience relativization' and involves a powerful actor disclaiming responsibility on the grounds that something was 'just an experience'. For example, a person in power, accused of abusing their position or offending others, might say, 'I'm sorry if anyone found my behaviour offensive.' This is not a sincere expression of regret – let alone an apology – because it doesn't relate to the individual's own actions. The person in a position of power is merely vexed at what someone else has experienced. The problem is relativized to being someone else's subjective experience.

The second way might be called 'experience absolutism', as it makes the very fact of a person's experience an unquestionable foundation for understanding and complying. Relativism and absolutism are, of course, opposing philosophical positions. However, in this context they are, in effect, two sides of the same experience coin. In the following sections, I will argue that in moral discussions, it is wise to have other coins available, ones that don't reduce ethics (and our ideas about what is right and reasonable) to experiences, and I will advocate the necessity of a more objective form of ethics.

Experiential Relativization

The term 'experience relativization' may not be common usage (at least not according to Google), but I use it to describe the tendency to dismiss criticism because it is just a subjective experience. I assume many readers will have found themselves criticizing something only to be told that 'that's just how you see it.' This form of dismissal usually reflects an unequal power relationship, in which the stronger party seeks to belittle the weaker's criticism due to it being a subjective experience. In other words, it's about the person having the experience rather than the thing being experienced. The problem with this reaction is not that every speaker and critic is based somewhere and observes the world from that position. That's just a basic fact. All criticism must come from a particular perspective, be it mine or yours. However, that is not to say that criticism can only be about what an individual experiences.

For example, if I want to complain to an airline about unreasonable treatment on a flight, it is the actual treatment I wish to question, not my experience of it. However, encouraging feedback on the 'travel experience' rather than the journey relativizes any criticism, reducing it to a subjective perception. It is worth remembering that, in many cases, it is utterly uncontroversial that a criticism relates to more than just the critic's experience. If I am walking along the street minding my own business and somebody attacks me, I report it to the police. It would be strange if they relativized the crime by being concerned only with how I experienced it. What makes something a crime is not that I experience the situation in a certain way. Something is an offence because it is wrong, illegal, immoral and the like – not just because it gives rise to an experience. An assault is still a crime even if I fainted first and was beaten up while unconscious. Being assaulted is not just an experience; it is a physical act, a violation of the victim. Hopefully, no one would dream of relativizing the nature of the assault into something subjective: 'It's only an assault because you feel it's an assault.'

In many contexts, that is precisely what happens. In several of his books, the sociologist Rasmus Willig has documented how critical voices are often swept aside on the grounds that there is something wrong with the critic. He describes this as a criticism making a U-turn, such that a criticism of something out there in the world – conditions in society, school or the workplace, for example – rebounds on the critic, who is told to critique themselves instead. As Willig writes, 'when you point out something criticizable in the world, there are always more fingers pointing back at you.'

Several lengthy passages in Willig's book *Afvæbnet kritik* (Disarmed Criticism) soberly list examples of rhetorical devices that disarm criticism by turning it around on the critic. His twenty-plus densely written pages make for quite a hair-raising read. Here are just four of the many examples:

1. 'You're the only one who thinks there's a problem.'
2. 'You need to see challenges, not problems.'
3. 'That's because you don't understand.'
4. 'I hear what you're saying, but that's not my experience.'[1]

The first retort clearly relativizes the problem, reducing it to the critic's experience. However, the fact that the critic is the only one to hold a particular view is not in itself a reason to sweep it aside. It may well be that the critic's view of the situation is legitimate and correct (or not, of course). The point is that you only discover the truth of a matter by looking into it. The issue is not the critic's experience (which is purely subjective) but what they are trying to point out. If you believe you are being discriminated against because of your gender, skin colour or disability and say so out loud, what needs to be investigated isn't just your inner experience of being discriminated against but whatever discriminatory actions and conditions may be at the root of the problem.

The second sentence is reminiscent of the attempts at positive reframing, as described in Chapter One – a strategy at which Donald Trump, in particular, excels. Talking about an issue in a more positive light, for example, as a challenge or a learning opportunity rather than a problem, shifts the focus away from the target of the criticism. Since there is no problem, nothing needs to change. Again, that may indeed be true – but you can't determine whether a problem exists simply by changing its label. You need to look into the issue in greater depth.

The third example refers to a shortcoming of the critic – a lack of understanding – which means we don't need to take them seriously. The fourth and final retort is a straightforward statement that when something is not *my* experience but *yours*, I don't need to bother with it. 'I hear what you're saying, but that's *just* your experience, so it's not that important.'

In summary, many of the strategies for disarming criticism in the experience society involve turning the critic into a problem, relativizing what they have to say and putting it down to subjective experience. If objective conditions are not the problem, but only the critic's experience of them, then what needs to change is the critic and their experience. You solve the problem by changing their experience, not by addressing the issue. This may involve, for example, changing the problem so it is no longer problematic but neutral – or even positive. In this way, disarming criticism is often linked to psychologization, where the issue to be addressed is the person and their inner experiential life rather than any external, objective conditions. Instead of management improving your working conditions, they send you on a mindfulness course so you learn to be present in the moment. You are asked to think positively, regardless of whether there is anything about which to be positive. You are told to reconstruct your thoughts or reframe the narrative of your experiences rather than change the conditions to which they refer.

Willig himself does not link the emergence of these ways of talking to the experience society, but I think the link is clear. In the experience society, perhaps the most common way to disarm criticism is to relativize a critical remark, to make it about some subjective aspect of the critic – that is, about their experience. In purely argumentative terms this is not on, of course. At the risk of repeating myself, to find out whether criticism is justified or not, we must examine the world rather than the critic's experience of it – because the experience itself is not up for discussion.

Experiential Absolutism

While experiential relativization dismisses critique as a subjective experience, experiential absolutism points in the opposite direction by claiming that a critical standpoint is valid based on reference solely to experiences. As mentioned in the Introduction, at one point the

University of Copenhagen's guidelines stipulated that an action was offensive if a person *felt* offended, which is highly problematic from a legal perspective because it reduces the question of guilt to a subjective matter. In a court case, it is not enough for the offended party to discuss their feelings. They must be able to point to actual offences committed, not just experiences and emotional reactions to misdeeds.

However, in the experience society, it is not uncommon to define various forms of offence based solely on how they are experienced, which positions feeling offended as an absolute, as beyond discussion. For example, one trade union writes this about bullying on its website: 'If you experience offensive and hurtful actions and cannot defend yourself against them, it is bullying. This is true even if the person subjecting you to the behaviour did not intend to bully you.'[2] Under this approach, whether bullying actually occurred is ultimately a purely subjective question. If I *feel* I've been bullied, I *have* been bullied. In principle, anything can be defined as bullying, which is a slippery slope to chaos because it then becomes possible to frame all sorts of subjective experiences as absolute truths.

Fortunately, other definitions of bullying refer to something beyond the individual's sphere of experience. For example, the Danish Centre for Educational Environment (DCUM) states: 'Bullying is behaviour that excludes one or more students from the community, intentionally or unintentionally.'[3] If bullying is rightly defined in terms of actions – and not just experiences – then it becomes possible to test the validity of claims that it has taken place. Bullies can be punished or apologize for their behaviour, and the chances of repairing the relationship between perpetrator and victim are far higher if the behaviour is discussed in light of what actually happened rather than solely on the basis of what was experienced. The chances of reaching a fair judgment – in schools, workplaces and, ultimately, the legal system – are also far higher if we avoid making experiences the absolute and indisputable basis for discussing transgressions and disputes.

I suspect readers may find my argument a little naive, given that there is often no consensus on what has happened in a given situation. The person accused of bullying might argue that it was just banter, the accuser that it was seriously and persistently offensive. It is clear that such divergent perspectives are common, and it is a part of the human condition that people see things differently in all sorts of contexts. The point is that both experiential relativism and experiential absolutism, by definition, negate the possibility of rational discussion about what happened because the two sides' arguments are both based solely on the subjective and emotional. The debate grinds to a halt when one party says, 'I felt bullied,' and the other says, 'I thought we were getting on well together and it was just good-natured banter.' Neither can be more right than the other because it all boils down to subjective experience. In the end, whoever argues their case most forcefully is considered right – which is not the same as actually *being* right.

If, on the other hand, you believe it's possible to make more or less accurate claims about offences and bullying, you need to break out of the prison of subjectivity and refer to observable actions. Remaining in the sphere of experience precludes the possibility of saying something correct, true and valid because, by definition, we cannot be wrong about our own experiences. If I feel offended, I feel offended. The experience is absolute because I am the first, last and only authority on how I experience the world and I am entitled to demand justice for myself and consequences for others on that basis. On the other hand, other people are always free to say that my experience was, by definition, just an experience. Relativism and absolutism are two sides of the same coin, and for that reason experience is insufficient as a basis for normative discussion of whether an offensive act or other form of problematic behaviour has actually occurred. When discussing questions of guilt, there must be a possibility, at least in principle, that we might be wrong.

Questions of guilt are often complex, and determining the truth is not necessarily easy. Nonetheless, the difficulty of seeking the truth about incidents and events is preferable to abandoning any idea of objectivity and retreating into a subjective space. We must teach our children – and each other – to analyse the world and events as soberly and honestly as possible rather than engage in a struggle to dominate discussions on all sorts of topics by claiming that our particular subjective experiences take precedence. The idea is not to ignore injustice and oppression but to talk about them as they exist objectively.

We must bring them into the light rather than leave them languishing in the dark realm of experience, where they can mean both everything and nothing.

Towards Objective Ethics

The fact that I have argued against experiential relativism and experiential absolutism doesn't mean I consider ethical discussions about offences and criticisms questionable or downright impossible. On the contrary, I think it is very much possible to discuss ethics rationally, even objectively, although this view runs counter to the widely held belief these days that ethics are subjective and there is no such thing as objective values. One of the characteristics of the emergence of the experience society is that it has taken place at the same time as the historical development of subjectively based forms of ethics such as emotivism and existentialism.

In such a short book, there is no way I can do justice to ethics and its history, but it is fair to say that classical moral systems such as virtue ethics (Aristotle), duty ethics (Kant) and utilitarian ethics (Mill) were swept aside by significant currents in twentieth-century moral philosophy, both in Anglo-Saxon circles and on the European continent. One of the seminal British texts reflecting this trend was A. J. Ayer's *Language, Truth and Logic* (1936), in which the author claims that, ultimately, all moral judgements are merely expressions of approval and disapproval.[4] For example, when we say, 'It's wrong to steal sweets from children,' we are essentially saying nothing more than 'I feel bad about stealing sweets from children.' The sentence simply expresses an individual's emotional displeasure at the phenomenon. In other words, moral judgement is based solely on a subjective experience of negative value. Conversely, when we say, 'It's good to help people in need,' it means nothing more than 'The thought of helping people in need makes me feel good.'

The theory is called 'emotivism' because it is based on the principle that feelings – emotions – underlie perceptions of good and evil, right and wrong. Moral statements have no truth value because, in a disenchanted world, there is nothing that could make them true. Ergo, they are neither true nor false, just as it is neither true nor false to laugh at a joke or cry during a sad film. Such responses are merely immediate expressions of emotion. Ayer and the emotivists believed this was also the case with human morals. Emotivism is sometimes referred to as the 'boo–hooray theory' because of the way it analyses moral statements. For example, it would reduce the Danish Council on Ethics' long, complex discussions on various issues to something like: 'Active euthanasia? Boo!' and 'Greater health equality? Hooray!'

Around the same time, existentialism, a philosophy that differed from emotivism in many ways but was quite close to its analysis of ethics and values, emerged in France. It is a far more nuanced philosophical tradition than I can do justice to here. Broadly speaking, Jean-Paul Sartre understood good and evil as the result of the individual's subjective choices – an idea that resembles emotivism. Existentialism, too, is rooted in the notion that the world is devoid of meaning and value. These phenomena, therefore, only exist as a consequence of human choices. As such, good and evil, right and wrong, become quite subjective.

Perhaps the most famous example of this in Sartre's philosophy is in *Existentialism Is a Humanism* (1946), in which he relates how a young man sought his advice.[5] Should he leave his sick mother to join *la Résistance* and fight the Nazis, or should he, as his mother's only close relative, give up the fight against the occupying forces and stay with her? In reality, Sartre replies, it is impossible to give the young man any advice. He has to make a 'radical choice', one that cannot be rationally justified. The radical choice is not a matter of taking into account different values (in this case, the survival of the fatherland and his duties as a son) because that would presuppose that those values existed prior to the choice. Sartre's point is that these values only manifest when they are chosen. In other words, it is the subjective choice of values that enables ethical demands to be placed upon people.

Whereas emotivism sees moral statements as mere emotional outbursts, Sartre asserts that individuals actively choose their moral values. However, both are ultimately rooted in the same subjectivist position – on what criteria should individuals choose their values, if not their subjective perception of good and evil? Sartre's famous slogan, 'existence precedes essence', means there is no human nature, no deity, no reason, no universal values nor anything else that determines a person's existential trajectory. There is only the individual, who has nothing to refer to in purely moral terms other than their own subjective preferences.

The two philosophies – emotivism and existentialism – were formulated in response to a world that no longer held purpose, meaning or value. Modern science disenchanted the world in such a way that good and evil – as well as the meaningful and meaningless – are no longer found in something objective but must stem from the subjective, from the feelings and choices of the individual. These days, we don't hear much about emotivism and existentialism, but not because they ran out of relevance at some point in the twentieth century. Quite the contrary – the concepts were deemed so self-evident it was barely necessary to call them by their names. In the emerging experience society, they became pop philosophies – the person in the street's moral philosophy. They were, of course, also met with criticism.

In *After Virtue* (1981), the philosopher Alasdair MacIntyre analysed these positions and concluded they are symptoms of a moral breakdown.[6] Since ancient times, moral philosophy and its norms have been expanded upon to help humankind realize its essential moral nature. However, once this essential nature is removed – when everything becomes an expression of free choice and social constructs – morality loses its foundations and is no longer justified, according to MacIntyre. Morals are linked to emotions (as per Ayer) or free will (Sartre). They are random and ultimately reduced to subjective experiences. Good is good because I experience it that way. Evil is evil because I experience it to be so. Who else is going to define good and evil? Nowadays, many would say that it is oppressive for someone other than the individual to define right and wrong (albeit probably without being able to answer whether this perceived oppression isn't just a subjective attitude).

At the core of MacIntyre's work, as seen in *After Virtue* and subsequent publications, is overcoming the 'experiential morality' in favour of rethinking human nature as an ethical starting point. Another important critic of both emotivism and existentialism is Charles Taylor, who challenged Sartre's example of his encounter with the young man.[7] It always makes for a strong argument when someone is able to use a philosopher's own example to arrive at a diametrically opposite conclusion. According to Taylor, Sartre overlooks the fact that values are at stake in the young man's dilemma (caring for a close relative versus fighting totalitarianism), values he did not create by making a 'radical choice'. It isn't credible to say the young man can freely choose these values or not, as they help determine who he is. If that were the case, he could simply declare one of the two values worthless, and the dilemma would be solved. He can't, so he seeks out the famous Professor Sartre and asks for his advice. According to Taylor, the example shows that the young man's dilemma stems precisely from the fact that he *discovers* what matters to him and the values on which his life is based. They are not just something he randomly experiences, feels or chooses out of the blue.

I have dwelt a little on emotivism and existentialism because these two views of morality were widespread in the modern world that took shape after the Second World War. I believe they can be interpreted as an impoverished form of moral philosophy rooted in a world-view that emphasizes the subjective and the individual's experiences. In a psychological sense, it is also a world-view that engenders loneliness because the individual has only their own subjective experiences on which to draw when judging right from wrong. MacIntyre and Taylor sought to formulate more objective (or at least intersubjective) moral philosophies, according to which moral values do not stem from people's subjective preferences (feelings or choices) but are normative for our preferences. Ethics and morality (which can be used synonymously – one is Greek, the other Latin) are not about what we subjectively like but what we *ought to* like. Are there reasons to like love, mercy, forgiveness, helpfulness and charity that don't just stem from something subjective in me? Those who do not reduce ethics to experiences would say that there are. There is something outside of the subjective sphere of human experience that makes demands of us.

There have been various suggestions for how we might underpin a form of ethics not rooted in experience. One familiar to many in Denmark is Knud Ejler Løgstrup's 'ethical demand'. Being called upon to help someone in need that you meet along the way is not just an experience. According to Løgstrup, it is an unavoidable responsibility that stems from a fact: that people's lives are entangled. Løgstrup called this 'interdependence'. In *The Ethical Demand* (1956), he famously states: 'An individual never has something to do with another human being without holding something of that person's life in their hands.'[8] In other words, one person inevitably has power over another, which gives rise to a demand – to use that power for the good of the other rather than for your own good. This is not just something humans feel or choose (if that were the case, you could just opt out, which is impossible). According to Løgstrup, it is an ontological fact – part of reality itself, in other words.

Of course, Løgstrup also believed that we as humans can make choices from time to time, but always within the horizon of a life that is given. Løgstrup writes in *The Ethical Demand*: 'To be an individuality, a self, implies that something is claimed of me. And this in turn means that the moment something is claimed of me, it is I who must answer for what I do or do not do.'[9] You must answer for what you do or do not do – indeed, that is the basic condition of existence. But you cannot choose whether a demand is made, that is, whether something is demanded of you. The demand exists, regardless of whether you experience it or not.

Løgstrup's concept of interdependence doesn't just say humans have relationships with each other, which would be profoundly banal; it says we are dependent on each other. There are both positive and negative aspects to this. The negative aspect is that we can ruin each other's lives, and interdependence entails an ethical demand to avoid doing that. The positive side is that we can accommodate the other, help the other, and use our power over them for their benefit. From this positive aspect arises what Løgstrup later called 'sovereign manifestations of life'.[10] This original concept refers to how phenomena like trust, compassion and sincerity exist in our lives without us deciding they do. They are not subjective experiences or chosen conventions we can disregard or amend for the sake of convenience. For example, trust takes precedence over distrust, but not because of a democratic vote – it's just how the phenomena play out in reality. This continues to be the case even if a person has been disappointed so many times that their primary experience is one of distrust. This is because the very phenomenon of distrust only makes sense in the context of the trust that should be there but is absent for whatever reason. Given these sovereign manifestations of life, we inhabit not just a world of experience but a world of existence in which humans all share the same basic conditions.

For Løgstrup, interdependence is the ontological condition for ethics. Ontology means the study of being, and interdependence is the fact from which the ethical demand springs. Løgstrup even believed that the ontological approach is the third ethical tradition, alongside the deontological (that is, ethics of mind or duty) and the teleological (consequentialist ethics, which takes various forms). In a way, it represents a well-founded ethical re-enchantment of the world, transcending the morality of experience and anchoring ethics in reality.

These brief remarks about ontological ethics (which stresses that the ethical demand originates in reality, not just an experienced reality) don't do justice to Løgstrup's philosophy or ethics in general. My intention here is merely to correct the idea that ethics is necessarily subjective.

The last word in this debate has not yet been written, of course, but it *is* an ongoing discussion. It began in antiquity, with the Greek Sophists, and found particularly striking expression in the eighteenth-century work of the Scotsman David Hume, who believed that good and evil could not exist in the world because it is value-neutral per se, which meant the two concepts had to be in the mind of the beholder. Emotivism and existentialism, the modern variants of this argument, went on to become the defining popular philosophies of the twentieth century.

The debate about ethics is important if, like me, you are sceptical about the positions I call 'experiential relativization' and 'experiential absolutism'. We need a form of ethics that goes beyond experience and makes it possible to argue rationally about values. We should not just begin and end by referring to experiences and the subjective if we want to question the adequacy of the problematic paradigms that underpin the experience society. Ethics is not primarily about how we feel but about how we ought to feel; it is about what there is reason to feel. Ethics concerns the judgement of our actions, not just the experience of them. Experiential absolutism is inadequate because it disregards the normative question about reasons and makes do with just saying that an experience exists. Experiential relativization is also inadequate because criticism cannot be automatically dismissed based solely on its subjective anchoring in an experience. Feeling offended may actually be the result of objective actions and actual events.

3

Farewell to the Experience Society

Having made it thus far, you may well be wondering what makes a professor of psychology so critical of the concept of experience. After all, is the discipline not the science of experience? Is it not about the subjective? Am I not shooting myself in the foot by taking so many pops at the concept? I will address this issue in the third and final chapter of the book. It is also probably the bit in which I will make the cleanest break with most readers' preconceptions. Specifically, I will argue that experiences don't exist – at all – and, as such, psychology should not be considered a science of experience. I will conclude by outlining how a better psychology might look – one that overcomes attachment to the concept of experience. This will take the form of a constructive discussion of ways of understanding humans that are not tied to categories of experience. Prioritizing truer and more edifying images of humanity than those bound up with the concept of experience may make it easier to bid farewell to the experience society.

If those ideas leave you feeling the urge to chuck the book in the bin in frustration at the author's stupidity,

I hasten to add that I (of course) do not deny that people experience the world. We sense. We perceive. We see and hear our fellow human beings. We pet dogs and cats, enjoy films in the cinema and gigs, and eat good food from time to time. But experiencing the world is different from having *experiences*, understood as subjective objects or entities 'in' our minds. The problem is that using a noun like 'experience' can easily seduce us into believing the word denotes something that exists somewhere, like an object. It tempts us to believe that experiences exist in our heads or minds. Or in our brains. And that it is these experiences that we are in contact with when we experience the world. It is that idea that I find not only false but harmful, and I would like us to leave it behind. What we experience are not experiences but aspects and characteristics of the real, external world. When we live, act, sense and move, we are not making contact with experiences but with other people, dogs, cats, films, gigs and food. We taste *the food* when we eat it, not our experience of the food. We get annoyed with *the dog* when it pees on the carpet, not with our experience of the dog. We dance to *the rhythms* at a gig, not just to our experience of the music. And so on. The following may well be difficult for those who have only ever known an experience society overflowing with the vocabulary of experiences; however, any serious critique of this society's subjectivist ideology needs to replace its habit of doubling up on the experience of reality with a truer understanding of how humans and other living beings are more directly present in the world.

About Qualia – the Qualities of Experiences

Both ancient and contemporary philosophers have tackled this problem under the heading 'qualia', a philosophical and psychological term used to describe the qualities of experiences, such as the taste of beer, the colours of the sunset, the sensation of pins and needles when your arm goes to sleep and so on.[1] According to some researchers, no matter how many physical facts science establishes about the body, brain, central nervous system and sensory apparatus, our perception of the outside world will always be bound up with subjective experiences (qualia, or quale in the singular) that cannot be described scientifically or objectively, for example, by mapping our brain processes. In short, the way it *is* or *feels* to have experiences is, at least in part, inherently subjective. Add to this the notion that our entire knowledge of the world consists of something purely subjective, in the form of experiences and their qualities, and it might be said that we never truly make contact with an external world or other people. My whole world exists only as an inner experience, and I can only speculate that there are other beings who also have their own inner experiences.

Thomas Nagel provides a classic defence of the point of view that there is something fundamentally subjective about our experience of the world. In a famous article in 1974, he asked, 'What is it like to be a bat?' He answered that it is impossible to know, partly because we lack the species' sense of echolocation, so can't know the qualities of its experiences. Nagel nevertheless claimed that there *is* a way to experience being a bat.[2] By way of contrast, he pointed out that there is no way of knowing what it is like to be a brick or a river because objects like those are not conscious, sentient beings. The bat is sentient, and that is precisely why there is a way to be or feel like one. Or a dolphin, snake or human. Some consider this idea of 'how-it-is-ness' as the main problem in consciousness research. How is it possible to objectively study something inherently subjective?

The discussion about qualia has been a central one in philosophy, at least since Nagel, although its origins stretch back much further. The debate pits those who believe that the subjective perspective of experience is fundamentally different from the objective, scientific perspective and cannot be reduced to it, against those who believe that a scientific perspective can also explain the qualitative dimensions of our experiential life.

Like the heirs to Wittgenstein's philosophy – as mentioned earlier when discussing the meaning of language – I believe that conceptual analysis offers the most fruitful approach to this discussion.[3] It should rightly make us doubt the idea that we can talk meaningfully about there being a specific way it 'is' or 'feels' to hear, see or smell something. Thus, the problem of qualia is a pseudo-problem based on false premises, and both sides of the argument are wrong. If we asked a random person on the street what it is or feels like to see a bench, a response like 'Great!' would be appropriate if they were tired after a long walk and fancied a seat. But if we asked for an answer to a philosophical question about qualia ('What is the quality of your inner experience of the bench?'), the person probably wouldn't know what to say. There is simply no specific way it *is* or *feels* to see the bench. There is no experience associated with seeing the bench other than being aware of it. To believe otherwise is to have been seduced by a problematic psychological view of knowledge. Of course, when I see the bench, I experience something different than when I look up at the sky, but that's because I am observing two distinct objects, not because of the existence of two different qualia in the philosophical sense.

Based on such an analysis of everyday language, we must question whether meaningful discussion is possible of a specific inner experiential quality associated with a given experience of something in the world. If we are to speak meaningfully about such qualities (or qualia), we must talk about them as properties of objects and processes that exist in the world and not in experiences. When I see grey clouds in the sky, the greyness is a property of the clouds, not of my experience. It doesn't make sense to say that an experience is grey – or not grey, for that matter. Objects like clouds can have colours, but mental processes or imagined experiences cannot. 'What colour was your experience?' is a meaningless question.

We construct this relationship between the seen and the beholder, in which the former is copied and observed in the latter's inner world, in line with the philosophical tradition of Descartes, Locke and Hume already touched on a couple of times in this book. This is where the problem of subjective experiences or qualia arises. If the relationship is constructed in this way, the problem becomes insoluble because then we are only ever in contact with our inner experiences, ideas or mental representations of reality, not with reality itself. As such, we can never make proper contact with the world. It also means we don't have to solve the qualia problem – it should be dissolved by showing it is based on false and confusing premises.

We must refuse to take the approach to knowledge that doubles reality as our starting point. There is, of course, no denying that our experience of the world involves qualitative characteristics. For example, something can be pleasant or unpleasant, funny or dull, but this is a matter of an individual's relationship with what they face, not with a mythical quale or inner experience. The sentence 'The comedian was funny' makes sense. 'My qualitative experience of the comedian was funny' does not. When we talk about a 'funny experience', we are really talking about having experienced something funny (for example, a comedian). We don't mean we encountered a particular internal object – a quale or mental representation – that was funny. Similarly, when I see a red postbox, it involves just one object – the red postbox – not an experience of seeing this postbox as well. What I see is the postbox, not an internal representation of it.

In this light, there is, therefore, no problem with qualia, as long as we start from the right place and leave behind the philosophy-of-consciousness tradition's way of addressing the question. In short, we need to break the bad philosophical habit of thinking of experiences as subjective inner objects. But how can we understand human knowledge and our mental life if we do that? Is psychology possible without experiences? As we approach the end of the book, I will offer some hopefully affirmative answers to these questions.

Psychology without Experiences

Although some people stick to the belief mentioned earlier that psychology has to be the science of experiences, that is by no means the case. Yes, a line of thought has historically postulated that the discipline is all about inner experiences. Roughly, it extends from Descartes in the seventeenth century to British empiricists like Locke and Hume, all of whom pre-date the coining of the actual term 'psychology' in 1748. Indeed, empirical psychology did not emerge until 1879, at Wilhelm Wundt's laboratory in Leipzig, Germany, where he studied changes in his subjects' experiences when exposed to a sensory stimulus. What the ancient philosophers called 'ideas' – meaning inner objects of experience – gradually became, after Wundt, the 'mental representations' of modern psychology, which neuroscience later assumed were localized in the brain in one way or another.

This is very much a simplified overview of the history of psychology, but despite the lack of detail in the presentation, the emphasis on experience has nonetheless been an important part of the history of the discipline. We might call it the 'mentalistic' approach to indicate that it conjectures the existence of a world of experience in its own right, which it is the job of psychology to study, just as it is the job of physics to study the external, physical world. When this kind of mentalism enters mainstream culture, we talk about 'psychologization' – the spread of the idea that people are basically defined by their experiential life, something purely mental, which modern psychology has explored.

In fact, other threads have always run through the history of psychology. One significant alternative approach goes back to ancient Greece – to Aristotle, specifically. For him, the defining attribute of human psychology was reason, not experience. He said that humans are rational animals (*zoon logikon*), and that the fundamental characteristic of the human psyche is our ability to think, make reasoned choices and thus be understood as both ethical and political beings, unlike other animals on this planet, which only possess simpler forms of mental life. For Aristotle, psychology was a science of life processes rather than experiences. It was the study of how living beings think, act and feel, based on a recognition that rational beings like humans necessarily strive to think, act and feel more or less *well*. In other words, psychological phenomena (thoughts, actions, emotions and so on) are understood within normative frameworks. Something is only a thought because there is a difference between thinking wisely and thinking unwisely; something is only an action because you can act well or badly; and something is only a feeling because you can respond in a more or less emotionally appropriate manner to the situations that arise in life. Without these normative differences between 'should' and 'should not', there can be no psychological phenomena at all because everything would just happen – like the orbit of the planets around the Sun or the ebb and flow of the tides. Following this line from Aristotle, it is not the experience that is the starting point for psychology but the activity or action. The human being is not a passive observer who experiences but an actor who necessarily acts more or less well. According to the Norwegian philosopher Hans Skjervheim, human beings are first and foremost participants in various situations rather than spectators experiencing them.[4]

This thread in the history of psychology, which stresses action and rationality over mental experiences and representations, and was well established by Aristotle in his day, has persisted right up to the present, and is now seen as an essential corrective to mentalism. In 1904, after the notion of psychology had spread from continental Europe to the United States, the founder of American psychology, William James, asked a provocative question: 'Does consciousness exist?' His answer – which still sounds surprising to this day – was negative. No, consciousness does not exist.[5] Just as I don't deny in this book that humans experience the world, James did not deny that humans are conscious beings. For example, there is a difference between sleeping and being awake. There is a difference between being unconscious and being conscious, between being inattentive and being alert. However, according to James, this doesn't mean there is an object, an inner world we can call 'consciousness'. In contrast to the mentalistic idea of consciousness as an inner space – a kind of stage on which experiences occur – James argued that what we call 'consciousness' is a function. He claimed that there is a difference between the world and our knowledge of it (although knowledge of the world is also, in some ways, part of the world) and that acquiring knowledge of the world means becoming conscious of it. In other words, consciousness does not exist, but there are ways of being in the world that are conscious – that is, actively seeking knowledge.

This neatly parallels my view of experiences. Just because we have the noun 'experience' doesn't mean that such objects or things (in philosophical terminology, 'qualia') exist in an inner world of experience ('the consciousness'). Experiencing something is a function by which, as thinking beings, we come to understand parts of the world and are able to report on them and discuss them. This brings me back to my basic point. When we pay attention to symphonies, wars and overcooked vegetables, we are in direct contact with those symphonies, wars and vegetables – not our experiences of them. In the age of psychologization, we have been led astray by the concept of experience and find ourselves believing that cognition is an introspective activity in which the subject is a representation of reality and not the world itself. Coupled with the basic subjectivist view of the experience society, we find ourselves burdened with a mentalistic perspective that has locked us into our own consciousness, understood as a world of experience. The purpose of this book is to liberate us by showing that this perspective is fundamentally invalid and more ideological than scientific.

Psychology without Psychologization

One definition of psychologization is extending a psychological understanding to all sorts of areas of life and society not necessarily best understood in psychological terms. In the experience society, as I tried to show in Chapter One, the spread of psychologization took its starting point in the idea of a subjectivist view of experiences. But can we have psychology without psychologization? Might there be ways of understanding our psychology other than locking people into their own subjective experiences? Of course there can, and I will highlight a few examples, all of which might be said to follow Aristotle's thread but have been refined in the modern era from the twentieth century onwards.

Understanding the World

One of the fundamental questions in the field of perception psychology is, 'How is it possible to navigate the world visually?' From around 1950 onwards, James J. Gibson was at the forefront of this branch of psychology, which studies how living organisms – primarily humans – understand the world around them. Rejecting the idea that cognition involves an inner world of experiences, ideas or mental representations of the outer world, Gibson developed an 'ecological psychology', according to which we perceive the world directly. He argued that perceiving is an aspect of life that is related to action and is not just an experience. It's not a matter of our visual perception consisting of us constructing a scale model of the world in our heads or minds, from which we then extract information. Gibson's experiments with perception psychology showed that we acquire knowledge of the properties of objects in space and time directly via how we move our living bodies in relation to them.[6] Information about the properties of the world is contained in the world itself, as it were, for example in the light that hits the retina of the eye. More precisely, we can say that information about the world is contained in the conscious organism's relationship with it, which is why internal mental representations are superfluous when it comes to explaining perception, according to Gibson. For example, how we recognize distances between objects can be explained by how we move in relation to them. If we step to one side and look straight ahead, things far away will appear to move relatively less in our field of vision than things nearby. This allows us to determine the position of objects in physical space and their relation to our body on the basis of purely optical conditions. We don't need to introduce an illusory 'inner computer' to calculate the distances. We perceive them directly without any need for mental representations.

In Gibson's eyes, it was not just simple distances and spatial positions that we perceive directly. He also described man-made objects and cultural artefacts as exuding certain forms of encouragement that could be recognized without internal representations. For organisms with two legs and a need to rest, for example, a chair represents 'sit-down-ness'. If you have acquired the physical habit of using chairs in this way, as the vast majority of people in our culture have, the 'sit-down-ness' of the chair is immediately recognizable. In this way, the chair 'encourages' use. It is not just something subjectively attributed to the chair because you experience it that way. Gibson called this kind of encouragement or solicitation an 'affordance'. We are able to perceive the meaning of objects directly because we have bodies formed to explore the world actively on the basis of certain habitual patterns of action. If you have experience of eating situations in Western countries, you will immediately recognize the importance of the knife and fork as tools that facilitate the consumption of food. We don't need to compare the sight of the knife and fork with mental representations of them to figure out what they are for. The tools have this function, which is not just an experience but something real, a part of external reality that cannot be reduced to something subjective.

Since Gibson, other psychologists have continued down this path and explored all kinds of cognition without referring to inner experiences or mental representations. There are now scientific societies and journals dedicated to ecological psychology. In this context, the word 'ecological' is not about looking after nature (although they would certainly agree with such endeavours) but indicates that psychological processes and properties are understood as inseparable from the context – the ecology – in which they are embedded. In this perspective (which I share), perception and cognition are functions of actions in an environment and context (ecology) where things have meaning and reveal their utility through affordances. Cognition is not a matter of passively absorbing sensory impressions and forming inner experiences. It is linked to the movements of the body and the whole organism's active exploration of the real world around them.

Understanding Others

It is one thing for ecological psychology to point out that we can perceive distances, tables, chairs, knives and forks in the world around us. But there is something else that it's crucial for us to understand – other people. In fact, understanding other people is probably the most essential part of human existence. How do we know how they are getting on? Understand their feelings? Read their intentions? According to many psychological theories, the answer lies in the mentalistic approach. We attempt to understand other people by imagining what it is like to be them. We try to copy or simulate the other person's world of experience in our own mind. To the extent that the two inner worlds of experience match, we understand the other. Many psychologists talk about a 'Theory of Mind' – a theory about other people's minds, which we build up over the course of our lives. At least, that is the case when neural development is typical. One (somewhat controversial) theory about autism is that people with this type of neurodivergence have difficulty establishing a Theory of Mind.

However, this model does not work if we perceive the world around us – including the presence of other people in it – in a more direct manner. Perhaps my understanding of other people does not have to be based on an imaginary reconstruction of their experiential life in mine. Indeed, the Theory of Mind model has come under heavy fire from ecological psychologists and others who believe it is misguided to think that we carry around in our heads a ready-made theory about other people's states of mind, thoughts and feelings.[7] The argument goes that, under normal circumstances, we can read people's states of mind far more directly. Just as we don't have a 'theory' about what the sounds mean when other people speak but hear the meaning directly via the words spoken (assuming that we have mastered the language concerned), we also understand the other person's grief when they cry in despair at the loss of a loved one. Or, to take a very banal and everyday example, we understand the other person's intention when they cut off the top of their soft-boiled egg and reach for the salt. Knowledge of what other people want, feel and think is often immediately apparent in their actions and speech acts in a given context. There is no need for a 'theory' to connect behaviour and states of mind.

This idea is also the starting point for part of the phenomenological psychology to emerge in the twentieth century. While they had their differences, the great phenomenological philosophers Edmund Husserl, Martin Heidegger and Maurice Merleau-Ponty all agreed that the world of human life should be at the centre of any investigation of our being in the world. As a concept, the 'lifeworld' refers to the reality we live in and experience prior to forming theories about phenomena. For example, love is an important phenomenon in human life. It primarily manifests itself in our relationships, emotions and actions; only after that is it a subject we study as a hormonal or neuroscience phenomenon. It only makes sense to investigate the physiology of love because we are already familiar with it as a phenomenon in the lifeworld. Otherwise, we wouldn't know it was worth studying.

The point of phenomenological research is to understand human phenomena based on what they mean in life as it is lived. The lifeworld is not an inner, private sphere of experience but a shared world of meaning and significance. Phenomenologists seek to describe this world as accurately and completely as possible. The lifeworld isn't just a subjectively experienced world but just as much a *lived* one with which we – and others – have a practical and pre-reflective relationship. We don't think about how we hold a glass when we want to drink, place one foot in front of the other when we go for a walk or kick the ball when playing football. In these situations, the body's intentionality of movement is at play, which allows us to recognize the properties of the world – including the social world inhabited by other people – without thinking about it. In this perspective, when we live, we are 'out in the world' and not 'in our heads'. We can also think reflexively, of course, and withdraw from specific situations in which we find ourselves. But that doesn't mean seeking refuge in an inner world of mental experiences. According to phenomenologists, everything mental or psychological exhibits intentionality, which suggests 'directedness'. In other words, our thoughts are directed towards actual conditions, our actions towards practices, and our emotions towards the value implications of our being in the world. As psychological beings, we exist in a condition that Heidegger, in his cryptic manner, hyphenated to 'being-in-the-world'.[8]

An Outward-Facing Psychology

Much more could be said about the understandings of humankind I have drawn on as potential alternatives to mentalism's experiential thinking. They stem from traditions as diverse as Wittgenstein, ecological psychology and phenomenology, but all share the belief that humans are fundamentally 'outward-facing'. We are born facing the world. From birth, babies engage in communication and action in relation to their caregivers. We move in a world we experience directly, via bodily action and interaction, without any need for inner mental representations. Ecological psychology has proven this. We understand the properties of things through our practical interaction with them in the contexts in which they are used. Heidegger made this a cornerstone of his philosophy, which did not require an inner world of experience either. We even (usually) understand other people directly – and when we don't understand them, it's not because our inner experiences of their intentions are wrong but because we don't yet know them well enough to decode them properly. Phenomenology, too, sees humans as intentional beings facing the world. Finally, as we saw earlier in the book, Wittgenstein demonstrated that meaning is necessarily public, as there must be a difference between using words and concepts correctly and incorrectly, and this distinction is based on a collective practice of speaking, referring and acting together. He argued that private languages are meaningless at best and impossible at worst, and that meaning is not bestowed on anything by referring to illusory experiences in an inner theatre.

These outward-facing ways of understanding people insist it is possible to understand meaning without experiences (Wittgenstein), cognition without experiences (ecological psychology) and other people without experiences (phenomenology). If we understand experiences as inner, private objects, they not only are unnecessary for the science of psychology but get in the way of a proper understanding of what it means to be human. If we accept mentalistic theories, we find ourselves with a lonely view of humanity, in which everyone lives in their own isolated experiential bubble. For that reason alone, exploring the insights afforded by more outward-facing views of the psychological is a relevant task.

In doing so, we may be able to use psychology to combat psychologization, which may sound paradoxical but doesn't have to be. Some approaches to psychology are not psychologizing, some theories of mental life are not mentalistic, and some understandings of how people experience the world are not based on reified inner experiences. That is why this final chapter devotes so much space to psychological alternatives. The idea is to show that psychology as a science need not be tied to the illusion of an inner world of experience. This means that the ideology of the experience society cannot be defended by saying that psychology has shown that everything is subjective. While some currents in psychology have argued precisely that, a number of other perspectives have shown that people actually understand the world around them directly and not just via subjective experiences.

Welcome to the Experience Machine

Some readers may remain unconvinced of the value of a picture of humanity that sees us as participants in a collective, real world rather than just spectators in a private world of experiences. For them, I have one more argument up my sleeve. It comes from the philosopher Robert Nozick, whose 1974 book *Anarchy, State, and Utopia* presents a philosophical thought experiment that, despite a hint of science fiction, isn't terribly far from the experience society in its current and future forms. I have written about the experiment several times before, but it's worth revisiting because it is an almost tailor-made counterargument to the tendency to think about life in terms of experiences.[9]

Imagine scientists have invented an experience machine, a kind of supercomputer that connects to the central nervous system via a sophisticated interface. When people are plugged into it, they experience whatever gives them the best possible life. The computer is programmed to deliver experiences that match the individual's deepest desires and preferences. A cycling fan can experience a life in which they win the Tour de France, become a world champion and perhaps even a successful commentator on Channel 4 once they retire from competition. Or you might become a world-famous painter, cure cancer or win the Nobel Prize. Or, at least, you might *experience* receiving the prize or being successful in other ways. The catch is that you're not doing it in reality, only in the machine. Your experience is so vivid that it is impossible to tell it's not real. Once plugged in, you forget you're linked to the machine. The process is also so complex it can't be reversed – you will never be unplugged again. Once in, you're always in and are guaranteed the most eventful and pleasurable life possible.

Would you want to be plugged into a machine like that? Anyone who has seen the *Matrix* films (a dystopian science fiction franchise in which humans serve as biological batteries for a supercomputer, which in turn feeds them with experiences) will be familiar with the dilemma. Pessimists might argue, with a grain of truth, that in our experience society, we have built something like a giant, collective experience machine made up of screens, media, interfaces, artificial intelligence, entertainment and all sorts of digital gadgets. However, it is still possible to switch off, leave the screens behind and go for a walk on the beach, which you can't do when plugged into Nozick's machine, which is always on.

Personally, I know I would never sign up for the machine. But why not? Well, first of all, I don't think the scenario is realistic. It is based on the idea of the psychological consisting purely of experiences 'inside the head' (that is, the brain), which I have rejected in this book. If there are no experiences inside our heads and we perceive the world via our movements, conversations and investigations into and of a shared world, then the whole experiment seems moot. We are not in our heads but 'out of our heads', as philosopher Alva Noë puts it.[10] However, even if we accepted the premise of the experiment and conceded that plugging into the experience machine would guarantee a long and exciting life, I still wouldn't do it. After all, the machine would only deliver the *experience* of living – not an actual life. At best, it would deliver maximum pleasure – understood as the experience of positive emotions and appealing events – but it would be meaningless, as there would be no actual opportunity to act (only the experience of doing so). Even if you could have as much subjective pleasure as possible, it would still not be worth it because you would have no opportunity to act in the world, no possibility of realizing objective human values. Perhaps this thought experiment, however fanciful, can remind us that there is a difference between living a life and experiencing one. The machine is designed to maximize pleasure and satisfaction, but I would suggest it is deeply and inherently unsatisfying to try to reduce reality to nothing more than how it appears to us subjectively. If I am correct, it again emphasizes how problematic the dominant subjective way of thinking has become in the experience society.

From Psychology to Society

Psychology, with its theories and views of humanity, is one thing. The society in which it exists is, of course, quite another. Perhaps the experience society would be unthinkable without the ideological foundation of experience-oriented psychology. But does this mean that all we need to do to leave the experience society behind is simply adopt other, less mentalistic psychologies? No, of course not. The experience society is a historical reality. It is rooted in consumerism, the attention economy and a huge experience industry, and has a strong technological underpinning. However, if this book's arguments are valid, this historical reality rests on an illusion and, in that sense, on an ideology.

As a result, several of the major problems of our day are, if not brought about by the experience society, then impossible to solve within its horizons. Most obviously, ecological crises – climate change, biodiversity loss and so on – which can't be reduced to mere experiences. In the consumer society, travel, entertainment and material consumption have been lauded as fundamental pillars of the good life, and that has depleted the Earth's resources. The resultant crises are objective realities we can't understand purely on the basis of the subjective experiences of individuals ('I remember extreme weather events from my childhood, so how bad can it be?'). If the experience society has exacerbated these crises but fails to present ways in which to cope with them, then it is all the more vital that we come up with a picture of humans and the good life that is not so exclusively linked to experiences and consumption. Of course, this picture must not deny that humans experience the world, but it must point out that it is the world, in all its diversity, that living human beings experience, not just an inner subjectivity. The good life rests on the realization that we are fundamentally outward-facing, immediately present in a reality we share with others and to which we are, therefore, obligated. We must maintain, care for and repair that reality. The world is not an experience. It is an all-encompassing reality on a scale far greater than whatever perspectives we might have on it. It is time to re-establish an understanding of humankind as immediately present and alive in the real world alongside other living beings. We are not separated from the world by experiences; we participate in it via our actions. Unless we acknowledge this, we have little hope of dealing with the major crises of our time, which require different ways of living, not just different ways of experiencing.

In Danish, we have two words for 'experience': one that refers to individual events and things that happen to you, and another that relates more to knowledge accumulated over time. It is to be hoped that a future experience society will place less emphasis on subjective one-off experiences and instead emphasize accumulated ones in the form of knowledge, skills and abilities. Such a society would not require people to abandon the idea of the subjective or the desire to know themselves, because people are, of course, subjects. We just have to understand that the subjective is always a perspective from which you view the world. It is a window on reality, not a mirror in which you see yourself. It is an opening to the world rather than a closed bubble. If we want to know ourselves, we need to know the world we live in, not just feel and sense ourselves inside a bubble.

Dare we hope that a different type of experience society – maybe even an awareness society – might emerge in the future? Perhaps one in which awareness is cultivated and trained in order to maximize people's interest in the world that created them and the other people with whom they share it? We gain accumulated experience by doing things and develop awareness when directed towards things in the world. Both are necessary to overcome the ills of the experience society.

References

Introduction

1 Gerhard Schulze, *Die Erlebnisgesellschaft: Kultur-soziologie der Gegenwart* [The Experience Society: A Cultural Sociology of Contemporary Times] (Frankfurt, 1992); Steven Miles, *The Experience Society: Consumer Capitalism Rebooted* (London, 2021).

2 Gert Biesta, *Verdensvendt uddannelse – et perspektiv for nutiden* [World-Centred Education – A View for the Present] (Aarhus, 2022), p. 78.

3 For a review of those aspects of the attention economy and its social psychology, see Vincent F. Hendricks, *Vend verden – genvind autonomien i en digital tidsalder* [Turn the World Around – Reclaiming Autonomy in a Digital Age] (Copenhagen, 2020). I also recommend Mads Vestergaard, *Digital totalitarisme* [Digital Totalitarianism] (Copenhagen, 2019).

4 The term 'real' is used here in the philosophical sense – that is, we live in a world that exists independently of us and is possible to know.

1 Welcome to the Experience Society

1 J. Andersen, J. G. Andersen and A. Hede, 'Tryghed og utryghed i Danmark 2021' [Security and Insecurity in Denmark, 2021], *TrygFonden*, www.tryghed.dk, accessed 22 November 2024.

2 Kasper Ellesøe, 'Kriminaliteten falder – utrygheden stiger' [Crime Down – Insecurity Up], *Sjællandske Nyheder*, www.sn.dk, 29 December 2021.

3 The word is especially used in the policy debates in Norway. For example, Øystein Blymke, 'I emokrati-land kan alt gå an – og følelser tar overhånd' [In Emocracyland Everything Goes – and Emotions Prevail], *Dagens Perspektiv*, www.dagensperspektiv.no, 16 August 2021.

4 Gwenda Blair, 'How Norman Vincent Peale Taught Donald Trump to Worship Himself', *Politico Magazine*, www.politico.com, 6 October 2015.

5 Carl Emil Arnfred, 'Peter Skaarup: "Fakta er under-ordnet vores holdninger og følelser"' [Peter Skaarup: 'Facts Are Subordinate to Opinions and Feelings'], *Politiken*, https://politiken.dk, 6 August 2017.

6 Støjberg was impeached and found guilty of violating the European Convention on Human Rights by instructing the Immigration Service to separate asylum-seeking couples in cases where one of the partners was under 18.

7 Stefan Nygaard, 'Jeg har sagt til flere af mine medarbejdere, at jeg elsker dem' [I Have Told Several of My Employees That I Love Them], *Djøfbladet*, www.djoefbladet.dk, 12 November 2018.

8 See my analysis in Svend Brinkmann, 'Det nye præsteskab – religion som Ritalin for folket!' [The New Priesthood – Religion as Ritalin for the People!], in *Medarbejder eller modarbejder – religion i moderne arbejdsliv* [Religion in Modern Working Life – Help or Hindrance?], ed. Joel Haviv (Aarhus, 2007), pp. 93–108.

9 Christian Stadil and Steen Hildebrandt, *Company Karma* (Copenhagen, 2007).

10 Richard Sennett, *The Fall of Public Man* [1977] (London, 2003).

11 Eva Illouz, *Cold Intimacies: The Making of Emotional Capitalism* (Cambridge, 2007).

12 Morten Ebbe Juul Nielsen, *Forbandede sunddom* [The Health Diktat] (Copenhagen, 2015).

13 Søren A. Kierkegaard, *Enten–Eller* [Either–Or] [1843], vol. II (Copenhagen, 1995), p. 170.

14 A. J. Barsky, 'The Paradox of Health', *New England Journal of Medicine*, CCCXVIII/7 (1988), pp. 414–18.

15 Svend Brinkmann, *Identitet – udfordringer i forbrugersamfundet* [Identity – Challenges in the Consumer Society] (Aarhus, 2008).

16 Ludwig Wittgenstein, *Filosofiske undersøgelser* [Philosophical Investigations] [1953] (Viborg, 1994).

17 Svend Brinkmann, *Standpoints: 10 Old Ideas in a New World* (Cambridge, 2018).

18 'Anbefalinger om brug af skærm' [Recommendations for Screen Use], Sundhedsstyrelsen [Danish Health Authority], www.sst.dk, 12 June 2024.

19 Steven Miles, *The Experience Society: Consumer Capitalism Rebooted* (London, 2021), p. 98.

20 For example, Guy Debord, *The Society of the Spectacle* (New York, 1995).

21 Charles Taylor, *Sources of the Self: The Making of the Modern Identity* (Cambridge, 1989).

2 But That's Just How *You* See It

1 Rasmus Willig, *Afvæbnet kritik* [Disarmed Criticism] (Copenhagen, 2016), pp. 91–3.

2 Business Danmark, www.businessdanmark.dk, accessed 22 November 2024.

3 Dansk Center for Undervisningsmiljø [Danish Centre for Educational Environment], https://dcum.dk, accessed 22 November 2024.

4 Alfred J. Ayer, *Sprog, sandhed og logik* [Language, Truth and Logic] [1936] (Frederiksberg, 1997).

5 Jean-Paul Sartre, *Eksistentialisme er en humanisme* [Existentialism Is a Humanism] [1946] (Copenhagen, 2005).

6 Alasdair MacIntyre, *After Virtue*, 2nd edn (London, 1985).

7 Charles Taylor, 'What Is Human Agency?', in *Human Agency and Language: Philosophical Papers 1* (Cambridge, 1985), pp. 15–44.

8 Knud Ejler Løgstrup, *Den etiske fordring* [The Ethical Demand] [1956] (Copenhagen, 1991), p. 25.

9 Ibid., p. 79.

10 Knud Ejler Løgstrup, *Opgør med Kierkegaard* [Confronting Kierkegaard] [1968] (Aarhus, 2013).

3 Farewell to the Experience Society

1 Svend Brinkmann, *Psyken – mellem synapser og samfund* [The Psyche – Between Synapses and Society] (Aarhus, 2009).

2 Thomas Nagel, 'What Is It Like to Be a Bat?', *Philosophical Review*, LXXXIII/4 (1974), pp. 435–50.

3 In line with M. R. Bennett and P.M.S. Hacker, *Philosophical Foundations of Neuroscience* (Oxford, 2003).

4 Hans Skjervheim, *Deltakar og tilskodar* [Participant and Onlooker] (Oslo, 1957).

5 William James, 'Does "Consciousness" Exist?', *Journal of Philosophy, Psychology, and Scientific Methods*, I/18 (1904), pp. 477–91.

6 The main work is James J. Gibson, *The Ecological Approach to Visual Perception* [1979] (Hillsdale, NJ, 1986).

7 I. Leudar, A. Costall and D. Francis, 'Theory of Mind: A Critical Assessment', *Theory and Psychology*, XIV/5 (2004), pp. 571–8.

8 Martin Heidegger, *Væren og tid* [Being and Time] [1927] (Aarhus, 2014).

9 Robert Nozick, *Anarchy, State, and Utopia* [1974] (New York, 2013). The most recent occasion on which I wrote about this was in Svend Brinkmann, *Think: In Defence of a Thoughtful Life* (Cambridge, 2024).

10 Alva Noë, *Out of Our Heads: Why You Are Not Your Brain, and Other Lessons from the Biology of Consciousness* (New York, 2009).

Acknowledgements

I first developed and presented the arguments in this book as a column in *Altinget* in May 2022, 'The Violation Debate Is a Superficial Expression of the Showdown with Our Shared Reality'. I would like to thank the editor, Christine Ploug Lindberg, for encouraging me to develop it into this more in-depth analysis. I am also grateful to Alfred Sköld, Lene Tanggaard, Rasmus Birk and Thomas Aastrup Rømer for reading and commenting on the manuscript.